Collins

EXPLORE ENGLISH

Student's Resource Book 6

Contents

About this book

This book is full of interesting texts for you to enjoy.

- There are good stories and plays to read and discuss.

Jane: Rex, I need your help! Please would you style my hair in a new and funky way, for the school end-of-the-year party on Saturday?

Suddenly, the head of a huge, slimy monster poked out of the hole.
The monster crawled out of the hole, roaring and growling.

- There is a wide range of interesting **information** to read and discuss.

Have you ever dreamt of living high up in the trees, like a bird?

Hello I'm Frank, and I work as an architect. In my job I design and construct buildings.

fashionblog/howto.com

Step 1: Do your research
Spend some time looking at other fashion blogs. What do you like? What don't you like?

This tells you there is something to **talk** about.

This tells you there is something to **think** about.

Enjoy the book!

I say

There is usually an editor's letter at the beginning of a magazine. Read this editorial column from a school magazine.

Welcome back after a long summer break! May the school year ahead be filled with happiness and success.

Take time to get to know yourself this year.

'Who am I?' When was the last time you asked yourself this question and really thought about the answer? How do you define yourself? Often in life, we spend so much time thinking about other people and defining the people around us, we forget to look at ourselves. We forget to think about how wonderfully unique we are. Learn to love and accept the unique you and, when times are tough, shout out this chant over and over again:

'I'm GREAT!
I'm COOL!
You can look,
But you will see,
There's NO ONE on this EARTH like me.'

You may not be the smartest in the school, but do your best, and follow my rules:
1. Work hard.
2. Play hard.
3. Don't follow the crowd.

Begin the year with a good attitude.
Pat yourself on the back, and shout aloud:

'I'm GREAT! I'm COOL!

And I can't WAIT, to start SCHOOL!'

Enjoy getting to know yourself as you read this magazine.

Your editor

Jenni Gallow

What is the main point of the editor's letter?

What does it mean to be unique?

What makes you unique?

Getting to know yourself

We all have characteristics that define who we are.
Read the characteristics in these diagrams.

Characteristics that define our identity

Beliefs

Values

Choices

Appearance

Objects, Possessions

Ethnicity

Identity

Creations

Practices, Habits

Interests

Work, Hobbies

Friends, Family

Which characteristics define your identity? Which are the most or the least important?

A personality word cloud

Which words on the word cloud describe you?

Psychologists are people who study the human mind.
They believe that we can be divided into three parts:

- the *real* me
- the me I *think* I am
- the me I *show* to others.

We should **be** our real self, **know** our real self and **show** our real self.

Are there times when you don't show the real *you to your classmates?*

Personality types

Think of three words to describe your best friend.
Now read about these four different personality types.

Yellow rays of sunshine

You have lots of energy.

You are playful, talkative and love to meet new people and laugh together ... the most important thing is to have fun!

You have many great ideas, but you don't always finish things.

You are confident and have many friends. Sometimes you are noisy.

You are happy and full of fun.

Which personality type best describes you? Why?

Purple carers

You are always friendly.

You care about other people and how they are feeling.

You want everyone to be happy and to work together peacefully and happily.

You are generous and kind.

You don't need to be the leader and are happy to work together as a team.

You are patient and helpful and don't usually feel angry.

Green go-getters

You like to get things done!

You are focused and enjoy finishing something.

You like to win competitions.

You are happy to be a leader and feel good when people do what you tell them to do, but you don't like to be told what to do.

You don't waste time and can be very honest, even if it is not always kind.

You sometimes feel quite angry when things don't go as you planned.

Blue thinkers

You like to think about things.

You like to know the facts, not just opinions. You look for the answers to questions that you don't know.

You are organised and neat.

You are usually well prepared, quiet and calm.

You might only have a few friends or one best friend.

We are all different

Is everyone in your class the same as you?

Of course not! That would be crazy!

Life is more interesting because we are all different. Just as it is important to know yourself, it is important to know about the people around you and to accept that you are all different.

When we learn more about each other, it is easier to feel empathy. Empathy means putting yourself in someone else's shoes, or trying to understand how it feels to be someone else.

When we empathise, we think about how our actions make other people feel. This helps us to be kind and also teaches us tolerance. Tolerance means to accept everyone, even if they are very different from you. If we have empathy and tolerance, we can all be friends and live together peacefully in our world.

How does being different make life more interesting? Share ideas.

Being fabulous

Read this comic about Paul's party.

Focus on... bullies

Bullying is a problem in many schools. Read this information.

Some people don't like who they are. They are unhappy and need to pretend that they are tougher than they really are. They also don't know how to show empathy or be tolerant of other people's differences. These people often become bullies. A bully is a person who uses their strength or power to make other people do what they want. The people they tease or try to control are called victims.

Bullies often take money, food or things from their classmates. They call people bad names and tease the children who are different from them. They sometimes hurt other learners or won't be friends with someone. They may tell lies about their classmates because they think this will make them more popular. Bullying is a very bad thing and it is important to always tell your teacher if someone is bullying you.

Why do people bully?

To pretend they are big and strong.

To try and make other people scared of them.

To try and make other people like them.

To hide their own fears.

They are copying other bullies.

They are unhappy.

They don't like who they are.

Have you ever been bullied? How did you feel? What did you do?

BULLYING

Physical bullying

Hitting, kicking, punching, pushing, slapping, hurting, taking your things or food.

Calling you bad names, threatening you, saying mean things, being rude, nasty and unkind to you, teasing you because you are different.

Verbal bullying

Cyber bullying

Using the internet to send unkind messages, tell lies about you, share private information or pictures, be mean to you.

Emotional bullying

Telling people lies about you, not letting you join a group of friends, telling other people not to be your friend, gossiping about you, ignoring you.

Good reads

Different types of stories are called 'genres'. Examples include: fantasy, mystery, drama, comedy, adventure, romance, horror, realistic fiction.

Read these two stories.

Which genre do you like best? Why?

Elephant's Ears

Elephant had gigantic ears that flipped and flopped over his eyes, but he was too scared to visit the ear dressers.

Goose tied his ears up with a pink ribbon, but that was too girlie.

Chimp made him a hat out of bananas, but that was too sticky.

Snail gave him his shell, but that was too small and fell off.

So he had to be brave and visit the ear dressers with his mummy.

Now he loves the ear dressers and goes there all the time.

Everyone says he has the best ear style of all!

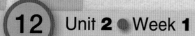

Harry the Clever Spider on Holiday

Harry was Clare's pet spider and he was very clever. Clare wanted to take Harry on holiday to Spain, but Mum said she couldn't.

'We need him to stay at home to keep an eye on things,' Mum explained. 'Besides, animals aren't allowed on planes.'

'Harry isn't an animal!' cried Clare. 'He's a minibeast.'

Harry didn't say anything, but he listened and watched.

'I'm glad that hairy monster can't come on holiday with us,' said Charlie. 'Don't think of hiding him – because I'm watching.' Charlie was Clare's brother and he was scared of spiders.

Clare did think about hiding Harry, but decided against it. She knew she would miss him a lot – and he would miss her. But she didn't want him to get into trouble.

She helped her mum put address labels on the cases.

'We don't want to lose them,' Dad said. 'We'll need our swimsuits for the beach.'

'And we don't want to lose the necklace Dad's going to buy me for my birthday from a shop at the airport!' said Mum, excitedly.

Clare felt sad driving to the airport without Harry. Then when they were in the check-in queue she felt something tickling her hand. She guessed who. Oh no! Naughty Harry!

'What are you laughing at?' said Charlie suspiciously.

'Nothing,' said Clare. 'Why don't you keep an eye on your things? Someone might take a fancy to your computer game.' But Charlie put his game away and kept a lookout for Harry.

Which genre are these stories?

Do you like stories like this? Why?

Good endings

Read the information about good endings to stories. Do you agree with the points? Now read 'The Monster of Pit Street'.

Good endings

- should bring the story together by tying up loose ends
- may make the reader feel a strong emotion
- may surprise the reader
- may ask a question
- may end with a mystery
- may share a lesson about life (a moral).

How do you think the story ends?

The Monster of Pit Street

The cellar was dark and cold.
'I don't like this place,' said Nick. 'It's creepy.'

Underneath the floorboards, there was more of the cellar.

The lower half of the cellar was dark and dusty. It smelt like old socks.

Suddenly, a strange growl came from deep under the hole. Nick's hands started to shake.

The growl got louder and louder.

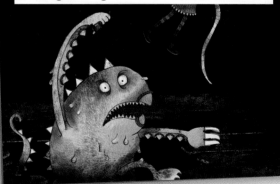

Suddenly, the head of a huge, slimy monster poked out of the hole.

The monster crawled out of the hole, roaring and growling.

Famous stories

Some stories are famous because people have been retelling them for many years. Others are famous because they have an excellent ending or teach a good life lesson (a moral).

While you read this fable, think about why it is famous.

The Hare and the Tortoise

Hare said to Tortoise, 'I'm so much bigger and better than you.'

Tortoise said, 'Bigger doesn't always mean better.'

They both said, 'Let's have a race.'

Hare thought he was so much better than Tortoise that he gave him a head start.

Hare ran past Tortoise. Hare had time to eat. Hare had time to play. Hare had time to snooze … He fell asleep among the cabbages. Tortoise slowly plodded past.

When Hare woke up, Tortoise had almost won!

Hare hopped fast, but he couldn't catch up. Everyone cheered as Tortoise won.

What famous stories do you know? Do they have a moral?

Changing famous stories

Sometimes writers like to change famous stories a little to make them more interesting. 'Jack and the Beanstalk' is a traditional tale that has been told for many years. Over the years, writers have changed the story in many different ways. They have changed:

- the characters: 'Kate and the Beanstalk'
- the setting: 'Paco and the Giant Chile Plant'
- the ending: the giant is catapulted into space in one version
- the way it is presented: a play, a poem, a song and even a rap.

Read this version of the story.

Jack and the Beanstalk

Jack and Mum were poor.

We must sell Daisy!

Jack sold Daisy for some beans.

Silly boy!

Mum was cross.

Silly boy!

A beanstalk grew! Jack climbed up and up.

At the top, Jack found gold! But a giant found Jack.

That's MINE!

Shall we swap?

The giant was happy. He grew a beanstalk too!

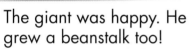

Mum was happy.

Clever boy!

How does this version of the story differ from the traditional tale? Which ending do you prefer? What other ways could the story end?

Fishy Friend

A boy called Kipp Whysall entered and won a writing competition when he was only nine years old. His story was published as a children's book. Read his book, in which he uses rhyme for effect.

Sam and his family went to the beach
with a net, a spade, and a bucket each.

Mum built a sandcastle, Dad dug a moat,
Sam fetched the water and Tom sailed his boat.

They needed one more bucket to fill it to the top,
But then something pinched Sam, and that made him stop.

Which words describe the genre of this book? Poetry, mystery, adventure story, non-fiction, fiction romance, fantasy.

A cheeky crab had crawled along and nipped him on his toe.
Sam bent down and picked it up, smiled and said "Hello!"

Sam and the crab played in the sea, they laughed and splashed together.
But then the tide came in and washed the crab away forever.

Sam searched and searched among the waves but couldn't find his mate.
"Time to go now," said Mum, "It's cold and getting late."

At home Sam emptied his bag ... And, clinging to his jeans,
He found his friend the cheeky crab, who joined him for baked beans.

How to make storybooks

Read these steps to learn more about how to write a good story and make a storybook.

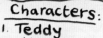

Ideas

First you need a good idea for your story.

Will it be a funny story?

Will it be a sad story?

Will it be a story about cats?

Will it be about sport, dancing or music?

Maybe it will be an adventure story …

… or a detective story?

Perhaps it will be funny and sad and sporty and scary!

Planning

When you have your idea, you can start to plan your story.

1 Make a list of all the characters who will be in your book. The characters could be animals, pirates, aliens – or they could be you and your friends. It's your choice.

2 Make a list of the things that will happen to them.

3 Think of a really good way to start your story.

4 Then think of a really good ending.

5 Then work out the bits in-between. You can change your beginning and your ending later, if you want to.

6 Make a good title for the book so that other people will want to read it.

Writing

Now you can start writing your story. Don't worry about making mistakes. What's important is the story you have to tell. You can write it out again later, or type it on the computer. If you change your mind about anything, you can. It's your story!

I must remember the 'ea' in treasure!

Editing

You could use this word instead.

Yes, that's better.

When you have finished your story, read it all the way through. Do you think it is good?

1 If not, make some changes to it. This is called editing your story.

2 Ask someone else to read your story. Do they think it is good?

3 Make some more changes.

4 Use a dictionary to check your spelling.

Illustrating

Do you want some pictures to go with your story? You can ask a friend to do them. Then you can do the pictures for their story – swap! Or you can do your own – it's up to you.

Now you have your story and your pictures.

Covers

What you need next is a good cover. This is very important if you want other children to pick up your storybook and read it.

1 Write the title of your book on the front cover. Then put your name as the author.

2 On the back cover you should write something about the book. This is called a *blurb*.

Making

When everything is ready, you can make your story into a storybook.

You could make it into a zig-zag book …

• a stapled book …

• a sewn book …

• or even a funny-shaped book.

Your teacher may help you to glue your story into a Big Book.

Discuss ideas for a story to make into a book.

Enjoying
Now it's storytime – enjoy!

Career focus

What does an archaeologist do? Read this information about working as an archaeologist.

What is treasure and how do you find it?

We're going on a treasure hunt, but how can we tell what is valuable? Gold, silver and gems are valuable, but what about animal bones and cloth? They may not look like treasure, but they can tell us how people lived long ago.

When something has been buried in the ground for a long time, it may change colour or shape.

Gold stays shiny.

Silver turns purple-grey and may break.

Iron turns into rusty lumps.

Copper and bronze go green.

Bones may crumble.

Cloth survives only in very hot, very cold and very wet places.

Anyone can find buried treasure, but you need an archaeologist to tell you more about it. Archaeologists study the past using objects that have been dug up. Buried treasure may tell us what happened in the past, when it happened and, sometimes, why.

An archaeologist's tool kit

trowel

sieve

On the dig

brush

pegs

string

When archaeologists found the leg bone of a cow it looked very ordinary. But when an x-ray was taken, 20 gold coins were shown buried inside it. This treasure was hidden, and then forgotten … for 2,000 years!

Why do you think someone chooses to become an archaeologist?

Look at the archaeologist's tool kit. What do you think each tool is used for?

Tough jobs

Read these job advertisements.

Sewer inspector needed

Are you brave? Does nothing scare you … not even bugs, rats, dirt or the dark? We have the perfect job for you!

Pipes that run underground connect all the toilets in our city. We need a sewer inspector to check that all these pipes are kept clean and unblocked. For this job, we will give you a specially designed suit and you will spend all day underneath the city's streets, working hard to keep our sewers flowing smoothly.

You can start as soon as possible.

APPLY NOW!
Send your résumé to: sewertunnels@jobs.ESL

Refuse collector wanted

Are you an early bird? Do you enjoy waking up before the sun rises?

If you like being out and about and on your feet all day, then this could be a job for you. No experience or skills needed, just a lot of energy and enthusiasm for keeping our city clean.

Positions available now so apply quickly!

Email your CV to: smellytrash@jobs.ESL

Plumber position available

Do you like a challenge? Do you not mind getting your hands dirty?

We have a plumbing job that is perfect for you. Our company is looking for a skilled and experienced plumber. You should be able to fix dripping taps, burst pipes and water leaks. Another interesting part of this job is unblocking toilets.

You must be available to work 24 hours a day, 7 days a week.

We're looking for someone to start next month.

Email us and tell us why you are the perfect person for this job: **funplumbers@jobs.ESL**

Call us for more information on 055 6784 132.

Are these jobs easy or tough? Why?

What is child labour?

Read this information about child labour.

Are there some days when you don't want to go to school? On those days it is a good idea to think about the children in the world who can't always go to school because they have to work. This is called child labour. Child labour happens in countries where families are very poor and children must work to help the family survive. If children cannot go to school, then they may not be able to get a good job in the future. So they will continue to be poor for their whole lives.

Child labour is not new. In the past, many children worked from a young age, usually looking after animals and crops. Then, in the 1800s, millions of people in Europe moved from the countryside into the growing cities to work in the new factories, and many children worked in dangerous jobs.

Boys as young as five years old worked as chimney sweeps. They had to climb onto high roofs and into small, dark, dirty chimneys to clean them. Some boys got stuck in the chimneys and others fell down them.

In textile mills (cloth-making factories), children had to clean machines while the machines were still running. There were many terrible accidents.

The new cities needed to burn coal to make steam so that machines could work. So children had to go underground into dangerous mines to dig for coal. Some worked for 15 hours a day in the mine.

'Powder monkeys' were boys, as young as ten, who worked on warships at sea, carrying the gunpowder to the guns in a sea battle.

Why were children used for these dangerous jobs in the 1800s? What can be done to stop child labour today?

What's new in travel?

Read this information to find out about magnetic trains and an exciting train trip to explore Vietnam.

Have you ever played with magnets? If you hold the positive and negative ends near each other, they snap together! But if you try to put a negative end next to another negative end, they push apart. Engineers have used this idea to build a Maglev train. Maglev stands for 'magnetic levitation' (levitation means 'up off the ground'). This train uses magnets to lift the train up and to push it forward. That means it floats above the ground … like flying!

The Maglev train doesn't touch the ground when it travels from one place to another. This has many advantages. First, it sounds quieter because there are no big metal wheels touching the metal track. Second, it can travel faster because there is less friction. And third, it feels smoother to ride on the train, because you don't hit all the bumps on the track.

Fun facts about Maglev trains

- The first public Maglev train opened in Shanghai, China in 2003.
- It cost roughly $1.4 billion.
- The top speed of the train in Shanghai is 430 km/h.
- In 2015, a Maglev train in Japan reached 603 km/h.

How does the Maglev train differ from other trains you know about?

Let's explore Vietnam!

Explore the beautiful country of Vietnam aboard The Vietnam Express on this highlight tour of a lifetime.

Travel by train from Hanoi to Ho Chi Minh City over six activity-filled days. Join us to see all the main attractions and wonderful sights of Vietnam from north to south.

Hanoi

Hue
Da Nang

Nha Trang
Ho Chi Minh

Itinerary:

	Arrival	Departure	Highlights
Day 1	Meet at Hoan Kiem Lake Hotel 9 a.m.	Depart from Hanoi 7:30 p.m.	• Hoan Kiem Lake • Ho Chi Minh Mausoleum • One Pillar Pagoda • Imperial Citadel of Thang Long • Hanoi Old Quarter
Day 2	Arrive at Hue 9 a.m.	Depart from Hue (the following day) 9 a.m.	• Tomb of Minh Mang • Hue Imperial City • Thien Mu Pagoda • Dong Ba market
Days 3 and 4	Arrive at Danang 11:30 a.m.	Depart from Danang 10:30 p.m.	• Traditional Vietnamese lunch • Afternoon on Non Nuoc Beach • Lady Buddha • The Marble Mountains • Museum of Cham Sculpture • Dragon Bridge
Day 5	Arrive at Nha Trang 8:35 a.m.	Depart Nha Trang (the following day) 8:35 a.m.	• Po Nagar Cham Towers • Night market • **Option 1**: Vinpearl Land Amusement Park • **Option 2**: Long Son Pagoda and Yersin Museum
Day 6	Arrive at Ho Chi Minh City 4 p.m.		• Afternoon city walking tour • Closing dinner • City nightlife tour

Education online

http://www.cityfacts.com

FIND OUT ABOUT CITIES   **WHAT IS A CITY?**

Sign in

WHAT IS A CITY?

A city is a large town. It is a place where many thousands or even millions of people live. Just over 50% of the world's population lives in cities. What is really surprising is that cities only cover about 3% of the world's land surface. That's a lot of people living in a very small space!

Most cities have three main parts.

The first part of a city is the **city centre**, where you can find banks, government buildings, museums and a variety of restaurants and shops. Many people work in this part. In the city centre you will also usually find a lot of tall buildings and skyscrapers.

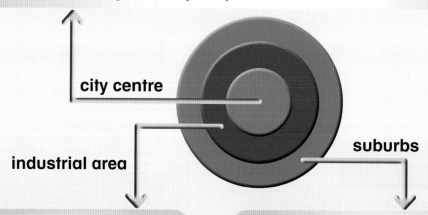

city centre

industrial area

suburbs

The second part of a city is the **industrial area**, where you will find factories and warehouses. Factories make things that people need or want, and warehouses store these things. Many people work in this part of the city too.

The last part of a city is its **suburbs**. Suburbs are on the outside of a city and this is where many people live. Suburbs don't have as many tall buildings but they have more houses and trees. Because they are further away from the shops in the city centre, suburbs have their own small shops and shopping malls.

In 2019 these were the tallest skyscrapers in the world. The buildings are ordered by roof or spire height, whichever is greater. Aerial measurements are not added to the height.

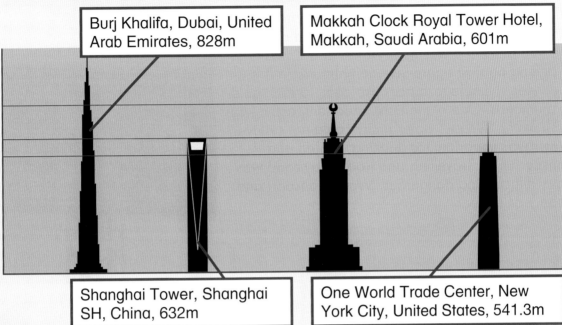

Burj Khalifa, Dubai, United Arab Emirates, 828m

Makkah Clock Royal Tower Hotel, Makkah, Saudi Arabia, 601m

Shanghai Tower, Shanghai SH, China, 632m

One World Trade Center, New York City, United States, 541.3m

Skyscrapers

Skyscrapers are tall buildings that have four things in common. First, steel or reinforced concrete is used to build a skeleton frame. The frame must be strong enough to support the weight of the whole building. Second, elevators are used to carry people up and down the many floors. Third, different floors are created for business, for living and for shopping or relaxing. And, finally, a skyscraper must be higher than it is wide.

Why are skyscrapers often built in cities? What are their advantages and disadvantages?

The Burj Khalifa is a skyscraper that is more than 800 metres tall. Wow! The tower was completed in 2009 and it took only six years to build. When it was finished, it broke the world record as the world's tallest building. More than 100,000 tonnes of concrete were used to build the tower. That's about the same weight as 50,000 elephants. Special glass was used to protect the building from the extreme desert temperatures and strong winds. It has 57 elevators that go up and down between the building's 163 floors.

Planning for the future

Old cities: In the past, most towns and cities grew without any planning at all! People would choose to live in a place if it was near water, or if it was easy to defend against aggressive neighbours, or if it was near valuable resources like coal, forests, gold or diamonds. One of the most important factors was fresh water. Without water a city could not survive. Water was important for drinking, fishing and transportation. Travelling and trading by road was slow, difficult and dangerous. Water transport and trade was easier.

Planning modern cities: These days, people are spending more time and money planning cities. Planning committees think carefully about water, electricity, sewerage, traffic, food, weather, schools, jobs and many other things. They think about difficult questions, like 'What makes a city successful?' and 'What is the best way to grow a city?'

City problems: Most modern cities all over the world have the same problems. Two of the biggest problems are pollution and waste. Traffic in cities causes pollution, and people throw away tonnes of rubbish every day. This can make cities dirty and unhealthy. Another problem is poor housing. As cities grow older, so do the buildings. It is expensive to build new apartments, so gradually the older buildings become shabby and broken-down. If there are not enough jobs, this can lead to an increase in poverty and crime in the city.

Chinese planning: China has a very different approach to planning cities. It doesn't try to destroy and rebuild parts of an old city. Instead it builds a new city in an empty space next door, or very near to the old city. This new area is designed from the beginning so it has better transport systems. There are luxury apartments and high-quality office spaces for people to live and work in. China has already built many of these new cities. Good planning means that there is plenty of space for a growing population.

Built-in technology: Mexico is planning to build a new smart forest city near the city of Cancun. Large parks, gardens and green rooftops will 'give back to nature' by absorbing 116 tonnes of CO_2 per year. Technology will improve life for people in the city. Buildings will have different sensors to monitor how much energy people use. By collecting this data, the city can help prevent the spread of disease and reduce energy costs. A system of waterways and water gardens has also been created. This can prevent flooding and is an eco-friendly way of travelling through this green, garden city.

Plan of the smart forest city in Mexico

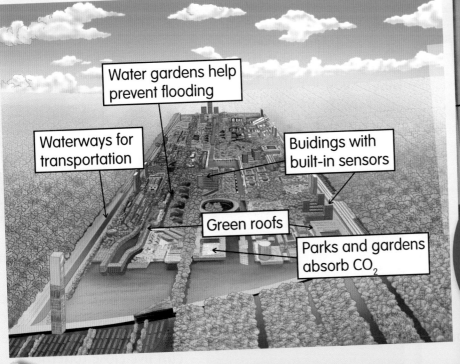

Water gardens help prevent flooding

Waterways for transportation

Buidings with built-in sensors

Green roofs

Parks and gardens absorb CO_2

Imagine you are on a planning committee. What changes would you make to your school or the area where your home is? Why?

Different homes

People all over the world live in a huge variety of homes. Even people who live in the same city live in different types of homes. Do you know what type of home you live in? Read on to identify your home.

Perhaps you live in a **mansion**. This is a huge and impressive home. It usually has many bedrooms inside. It might have a swimming pool and a tennis court in the garden.

Or, if you are a prince or princess, you might live in a **castle** or a **palace**. This is a large, grand home for royal families.

If you like to pack up and move to different places whenever you want to, maybe you live in a **tent**. You have to be careful of wild animals, but every day you breathe fresh air.

Do you live in a **treehouse** high above the ground? When you wake up in the morning, you can hear the birds sing.

It is possible that you live in a **flat** or an **apartment block**. This is a tall building with many homes inside. It saves lots of space in a big city and everyone can live close together.

If you live on the edge of a river, your house might be on **stilts**. This means that it is resting on tall, thin pieces of wood to keep it off the water.

Maybe your parents made your house themselves. If they used old pieces of metal, cardboard and other things, it is called a **shack**. If they used clay and reeds, it is called a **hut**.

Maybe you live in a charming, tiny house in the middle of a forest (or next to the beach). You have beautiful flowers in your garden and all the animals come to visit you. If this is true, then you live in a **cottage**.

If your house has an upstairs and downstairs, with your own driveway and garage, then you live in a **two-storey** house. If your house is tall and narrow, it might be a **townhouse**. There are many townhouses in big cities to save space.

Or perhaps there are two families living in the same house, with separate front doors. This is called a **duplex**. Every morning you can greet your neighbour when you go outside, 'Good morning!'

At home

A fantastic floating home

Imagine you could live under the calm sea, as free as a fish … well now you can! In Dubai, you could live in a beautiful 'Seahorse Home'.

This home has three levels. The bottom floor is completely under water. You can sit in your living room and watch the colourful fish swim past all day. It even has an underwater garden to attract magnificent marine life to your window.

Upstairs, there is a bedroom, kitchen, dining room, outdoor shower and even a jacuzzi. There is also a large, floating bed outside for you to lie on and relax in the scorching sun.

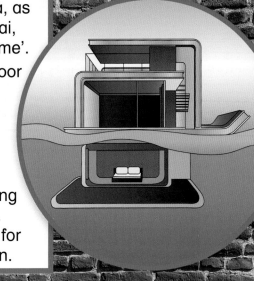

A luxurious home

If you visit Mumbai, India, you will be able to see the world's most luxurious home. It is called Antilla. A family of five live in Antilla – a husband, wife and their three children.

This home has 27 floors and cost around $1 billion to build. Every day, 600 people come to work in this home. They need to keep it clean, cook, drive, fix things and make sure the family is happy.

There is a ballroom, spa, private cinema and temple inside this house. It has many swimming pools and even a snow room, which spits out real snowflakes to keep everyone cool in the hot Mumbai weather.

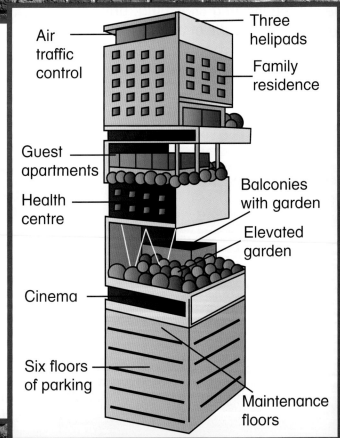

Air traffic control

Three helipads

Family residence

Guest apartments

Health centre

Balconies with garden

Elevated garden

Cinema

Six floors of parking

Maintenance floors

A treehouse up a trunk

Have you ever dreamt of living high up in the trees, like a bird? Well, if you were a part of the Korowai tribe in Indonesia, then this would be normal for you.

The tribe is very small, only 3,000 people, but the Korowai are famous because of their incredible treehouses. Some of their homes are 40 m high. This is taller than a 13-floor building. They choose to build their houses on stilts. This protects them from mosquitoes, flooding and keeps them safe if other tribes try to attack them.

The treehouses are made completely from nature. When someone climbs the ladder, the whole house shakes. Then the family knows that a visitor is coming.

In some big cities, like cities in Vietnam and Mexico, finding space to build a house can be difficult. It is normal to live in tall, narrow houses to save space.

In the scorching hot town of Coober Pedy in Australia, everyone lives underground, where it is cooler.

This upside-down house is not actually a home, but it looks like one.

What other unusual homes can you think of? Can you design one?

Building homes

There are many different ways to build your dream home. Some are made from natural materials like wood and bamboo. Others are made from shipping containers. It's even possible to 3D print a house with concrete! But some of the most creative homes, like the homes of Victor and Edouard, are made from recycled objects.

Victor Moore's junk castle

Victor Moore, a high-school teacher, writer and artist, wanted to build something interesting and different. So, in 1970, he started building a castle. He built it from things he collected from the local junkyard.

He used glass from car windows and washing-machine doors. He used old car parts and broken machines. He used pieces of rope, lots of wood and bits of metal. In fact, Victor was able to find a use for almost everything he found.

Now his castle is finished and it is certainly one of the most interesting recycled homes in the world.

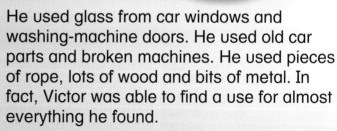

Some homes are made from shipping containers.

It's possible to 3D print a home in concrete.

Edouard Arsenault's glass houses

Another fantastic recycled project is that of Edouard Arsenault, who was born in 1914 in Canada. He was a fisherman who loved building things. One day he decided to build a house made of glass bottles.

In the winter, he collected different glass bottles from the people in his town. He cleaned them carefully.
In the summer, he started building the first glass house.

It took him four years to finally finish his project. He built three buildings from more than 25,000 glass bottles. That is a lot of bottles!

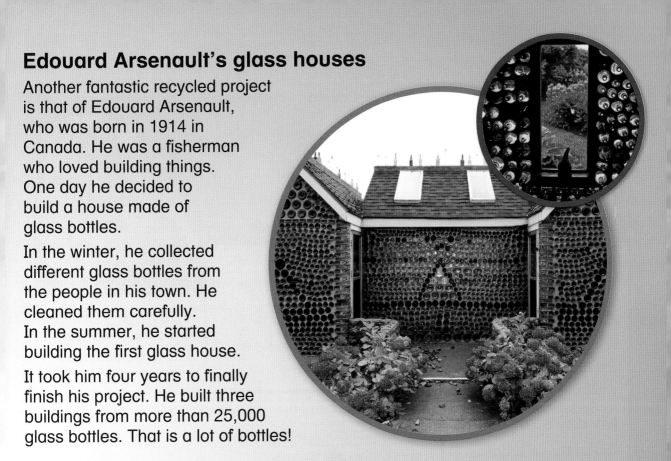

Next time you are about to throw away something that you think is junk, think again. Perhaps you can use it to build something wonderful.

Some houses are made of wood.

Some homes are made of bamboo

A Day on the International Space Station

Read about a day in the life of an astronaut, to find out more about living on the International Space Station.

I'm an engineer and an astronaut, and I live on the International Space Station. Life in space is quite different!

At sunrise ...

But which one? There are 16 sunrises and sunsets every 24 hours, so it is not easy to know when it's time to wake up.

Christina Koch is an astronaut. She spent 328 days in space.

My day starts ...

I go to the bathroom, and brush my teeth. But in space we cannot take a shower or have a bath. To keep my hair clean I have to use special dry shampoo. Then the team gets together to have a little snack for breakfast and a coffee before we start work.

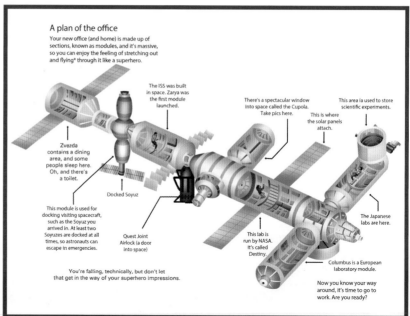

A plan of the office
Your new office (and home) is made up of sections, known as modules, and it's massive, so you can enjoy the feeling of stretching out and flying* through it like a superhero.

The ISS was built in space. Zarya was the first module launched.

There's a spectacular window into space called the Cupola. Take pics here.

This area ia used to store scientific experiments.

This is where the solar panels attach.

Zvezda contains a dining area, and some people sleep here. Oh, and there's a toilet.

Docked Soyuz

This module is used for docking visiting spacecraft, such as the Soyuz you arrived in. At least two Soyuzes are docked at all times, so astronauts can escape in emergencies.

Quest Joint Airlock (a door into space)

This lab is run by NASA. It's called Destiny.

The Japanese labs are here.

Columbus is a European laboratory module.

You're falling, technically, but don't let that get in the way of your superhero impressions.

Now you know your way around, it's time to go to work. Are you ready?

Meet the team

Oleg Skripochka (Russia)

Christina Koch (USA)

Andrew Morgan (USA)

Luca Parmitano (Italy)

Alexander Skvortsov (Russia)

Jessica Meir (USA)

Work ...

There are two main jobs on the space station. First, we must make sure that everything works and fix anything that breaks. Second, we run lots of different experiments. This is the part that I love the most! For example, we ran an experiment to grow green vegetables and Luca tried baking choc-chip cookies. They were quite tasty!

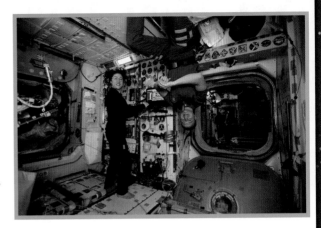

Exercise ...

In space there is no gravity, and this can cause your muscles and bones to become weaker. Astronauts have to do at least two hours of exercise every day to keep fit and strong. It's also a nice break from work.

Supper time ...

Most of the food is freeze-dried, so we just need to add a little water, and then it is ready to eat. There are no chairs or tables. Imagine floating around the room while you eat. But you have to be very careful and bring food to your mouth slowly, so it doesn't accidentally float away.

Bedtime ...

At the end of the day it's time to close the shutter on your window and put on an eye mask, so that the light doesn't wake you. You also have to clip your sleeping bag to opposite sides of the room, so you don't float around and bump into things. It's been a long Earth Day and it's time to say goodnight!

Real people, real problems

Read this information about refugees.

Refugees are people who have to move away from their homes because it has become unsafe or unhealthy to live there. Sometimes a natural disaster forces people to move away and sometimes people also leave their homes because of war.

Natural disasters such as earthquakes, floods, tsunamis or droughts can destroy homes and make places very unhealthy and unsafe to live in. People lose their homes and often family, friends, crops and animals as well. This can be devastating. These people need to move; to try and start a new life in a new place, even though they never planned this.

Some of them stay in refugee camps while other people go to other countries to look for better places to live.

These families in Turkey had to move into a refugee camp when an earthquake destroyed their homes.

Refugee camps are places where people can live safely if they have left their home or country.

Life in a refugee camp is difficult because there are usually no jobs and nothing fun to do. Refugees often have to live in tents which are not as comfortable as their homes. Many refugees hope one day to be able to return home.

Read this information about some ways people are helping improve the lives of refugees, and making more people aware of the problems refugees face.

What do you think it must be like to be a refugee? What emotions would you feel?

FILM

Refugee Kids: One Small School Takes On The World

This short documentary is about 120 students from 20 different countries at a New York City summer programme for children seeking asylum. The film tells of the children's challenges, trauma and triumphs as they resettle in a foreign country.

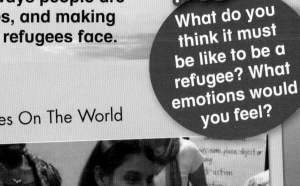

MUSIC VIDEO

Running (Refugee Song)

This song was released on World Refugee Day. It features Grammy Award-winning singer Gregory Porter, and Academy Award-winning rapper and actor Common.

It was recorded to create awareness and raise funds from people downloading the song to support refugees worldwide.

Book

Four Feet, Two Sandals

Lina and Feroza, two girls in a refugee camp in Pakistan, each find one sandal when relief workers drop off a bag of clothing. The girls meet and decide to share the sandals. As their friendship develops, they share why they have come to the refugee camp. You can learn more about how it feels to be a child in a refugee camp as you read about the girls' experiences.

Real people, real stories

Hanaa is nine years old and comes from a country where there is a war. Her hometown has been damaged and it is no longer safe for the people who live there.

Hanaa's family, including her parents, her grandparents and her two-year-old brother, managed to escape from their hometown and travelled a very long way. They then had to face a very dangerous boat voyage. Hanaa said: 'We had to go in a boat and I was really scared because the sea was rough.

Hanna was brave. She didn't want to go back to her hometown and neither the sea nor her fear could change her mind.

Hanaa and her family made it across the sea safely and are now staying in a refugee camp in Europe.

Hanaa's mother spoke about how relieved she is to see her children enjoying life again.

'Here in the camp some things are difficult for us, of course, but the children can go to the camp school and play football and feel safe. We are ready to start a new life.

'We hope we can go home one day, but for now we are very happy to be here and to be safe.'

Moving on

Look at the diagram. It shows some reasons that make people want to leave their home and move to a new place.

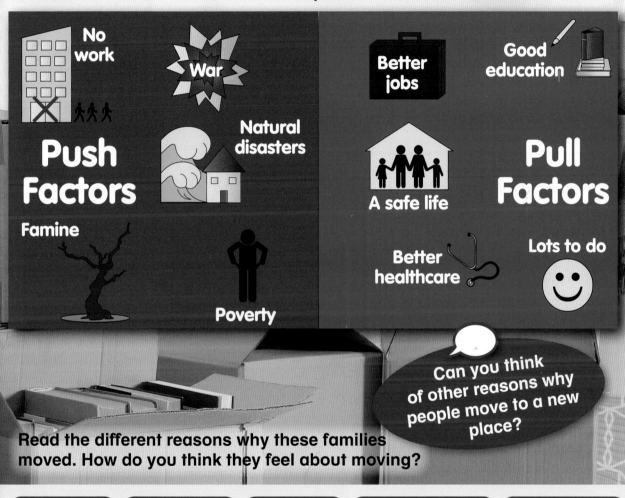

Push Factors
- No work
- War
- Natural disasters
- Famine
- Poverty

Pull Factors
- Better jobs
- Good education
- A safe life
- Better healthcare
- Lots to do

Can you think of other reasons why people move to a new place?

Read the different reasons why these families moved. How do you think they feel about moving?

We moved here to be closer to my grandparents. They are always very nice to my brother and me.

Anya

We had to move because it was not safe in my country. Here I can go outside and play in the park. It's great!

Max

We came to this city so I could go to a good school, but I'm going to miss all my old friends.

Ollie

Our house was destroyed in a flood, so we moved to the city. Our new apartment is really small and I have to share my room with my sister.

Elsa

My dad found a great job in the city, so we moved. There are so many shops and museums here to explore. I can't wait!

Adnan

I'm a designer

Read about these different types of designers and what they do.

Product designer

Hi, I'm Maria and I'm a **product designer**. I draw, plan and create new products for companies. Recently I have been designing kitchen items, like can openers and electric kettles. In my job it is important that the design is easy to use and that it works well.

Fashion designer

Hi, I'm Francesca. I'm a **fashion designer** and I love working with materials and designing clothes. In my job it is important to think about colours, shapes and patterns. You also need to understand textures and how materials feel when you wear them.

Graphic designer

I'm Ed. I work as a **graphic designer**. In my job I must communicate information using pictures and letters. I spend most of my time creating advertisements or packaging for new products. As a graphic designer it's important to have good drawing skills and computer skills.

Interior designer

Hello, I'm Saskia. I work as an **interior designer**. My job is to design and decorate the inside of buildings. I can work for private homes, hotels, restaurants or for big businesses. As an interior designer you must be good at matching colours, furniture and materials.

Animator

I'm Juan and I'm an **animator**. My job is to draw characters. That sounds easy but you need to be very creative and patient. It is difficult to give each character a different personality and to make them move differently. You must be very good at drawing and also using computers to draw.

Which of these design jobs sound interesting to you? Why?

Architect

Hello, I'm Frank, and I work as an **architect**. In my job I design and construct buildings. Buildings can be very expensive, so you have to be good at planning and working with money. You also need to think about safety, to make sure your building doesn't fall down.

Young entrepreneurs

Read about two young entrepreneurs who were inspired to create new designs at a young age.

Hart Main, the 14-year-old founder of 'ManCans', began selling manly-scented candles in November 2010. He started his business as a joke. His sister was making candles for a school market. He said the candles smelled too girlie, and that she should make manlier-smelling candles. His parents told him he should try doing it.

Hart spent $100 buying wax and scents online. Two of the first scents he chose were *Coffee* and *Fresh Cut Grass*. Now the scents he offers include *Sawdust*, *Campfire*, *Grandpa's Pipe*, *New York Style Pizza* and *Dirt*. He creates new scents when they are requested. Hart says that he has had some odd requests, like cow manure, but when asked if he was going to create this smelly scent he replied, 'Um, no.'

Hart made the candles in recycled soup cans. But he was making candles faster than he was eating the soup. So he donated the soup to soup kitchens, to help feed homeless and poor people. Now every time someone buys one of his candles, a homeless person also gets a warm meal.

Hart started marketing his ManCans by walking into shops and saying, 'I made these candles, can you sell them in your store?' A lot of stores said 'Yes', but many said 'No'. Most of his sales come from his online store.

Read the story of Kenneth Shinozuka and his grandfather. When he was only 15 years old, Kenneth designed something very special and important to help his grandfather.

When he was very young, Kenneth Shinozuka loved going for walks with his grandfather. One day they were walking in a park when suddenly his grandfather couldn't remember where they were. They were lost. That is when Kenneth's family realised that their grandfather had Alzheimer's disease. People with Alzheimer's disease often forget things and cannot make new memories.

Kenneth was very worried about his grandfather. He got his idea for a design one night. His grandfather climbed out of bed in the middle of the night and went for a walk. This could be dangerous if his grandfather couldn't remember where he was going. Kenneth said, 'As soon as he stepped onto the floor, I had a sort of "light bulb" moment ... sort of a "eureka" moment.'

Kenneth decided to design a sock with a sensor inside. He faced three challenges:
- First, the material for the sensor had to be thin enough to be comfortable on the bottom of the foot.
- Next, he had to design a wearable wireless circuit.
- Finally, he had to design an app that would change a smartphone into a monitor. The sensor connects to a smartphone app, which can wake the family up if their grandfather gets out of bed.

Now the family don't have to worry about their grandfather getting lost or injured, because they can check on their phones to see where he is if he goes somewhere on his own.

Think about someone you know who needs help with something. What product could you design to help him or her?

The Design Thinking Process

The Design Thinking Process is a method that some designers use to help solve difficult problems. An important question in this process is, 'What does the user really need?' Read about the five basic steps in this process.

Empathise
Speak to the user or customer. Find out their needs and what they like or dislike.

Define
When you understand the user, create a profile of who they are and what they need.

Ideate
Brainstorm different solutions. Think of as many creative ideas as possible.

Prototype
Choose two of your ideas and build them from cardboard, tin cans, plastic or anything you can find. The prototype helps other people to understand your idea.

Test
Show your prototype to your user. This is a chance to learn more about their needs. What do they like or dislike about your idea?

Design & Win!

The challenge
Design the perfect chair for one of these people:

Grandpa Donald has a bad back. He walks slowly and uses a walking stick to help him to keep his balance. He likes to sit and read books and watch TV in his armchair, but it is difficult for him to sit down and stand up from the chair.

Ramnik is a 12-year-old boy with a big, heavy school backpack. He and all the other students have to put their backpacks on the floor next to their hard, wooden chairs. Ramnik finds his backpack very heavy to lift up and down when he needs to take things out and put them away again.

Lily is a one-year-old baby and can't walk or talk yet. She spends all day sleeping or crawling around, exploring and trying to touch everything she sees. She doesn't like to sit in one place for too long. If she does, she starts to cry.

GRAND PRIZE: A trip to Disney World

Eight runner-up prizes: Designing books and equipment

Download your entry form:
www.designopportunitiestowinE2L.com

Enter in one of these age categories:

6–8 years

9–11 years

12–13 years

Energy issues

How can you use less energy?

Read these energy facts.

- On average, a plate of food in the USA has travelled **2,400 km** from the farm to the plate.

- One bus carries as many people as **40 cars**!

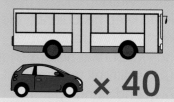

- Paper products have used up more than **one third** of the world's wood resources.

- Every year, we throw away about **45 million tonnes** of electrical waste globally. That means that by the end of January, we have already filled up four million buses with old computer equipment, TVs, phones and appliances!

- In the UK, around 500 million plastic bags are used each week. Less than 5% of them have been recycled. The rest will take **1,000 years** to decompose in landfills.

- There are about **6.6 billion** phones being used around the world. On average, we change our phones every **18 months** and just throw away our old ones.

- The average person produces **2 kg** of waste every day … that's a lot of rubbish from each family in a year!

The boy who harnessed the wind

William Kamkwamba was born in 1987, in Malawi. He grew up in a village that suffered from drought and famine. William's family could not afford his school fees, so he was forced to leave school when he was 14. William started borrowing books from a community library so he could educate himself.

William dreamed of providing his community with electricity and running water; two basic needs that only 2% of Malawians could enjoy. After reading about windmills in a book called *Using Energy*, William set about building a windmill out of scrap metal, spare parts and wood. His first windmill powered four lights and charged his neighbours' mobile phones. Later the windmill was made bigger so it could catch the wind above the trees. He built another windmill that turned a water pump.

William has written a book, *The Boy Who Harnessed the Wind*. This book and a documentary film called *William and the Windmill* tell the story of William's dream to change the lives of the people in his community.

William Kamkwamba's other community projects include:

- solar power and lighting for the six homes in his family compound
- a deep water well with a solar-powered pump for clean water
- malaria prevention
- a drip irrigation system.

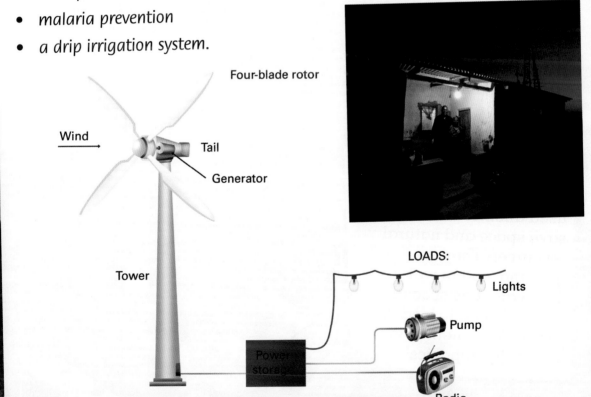

Looking to the future

We will need to produce more food in the next 50 years than we have in the last 10,000 years! Read this information to find out about some solutions to this problem.

The number of people in the world is growing and we are eating more food than ever before. This means that we need to stop wasting so much food! We also need to think of new ways to grow more food using less space and fewer resources.

Farmers have learned how to grow more food using the same amount of space. They are building vertical farms where layers of food grow on top of each other. These farms are usually indoors, where the farmers can control the environment to grow the largest amount of food possible.

Farmers have also used another method to save space and natural resources. They are growing food in water. The water has special minerals in it to feed the plants. This method is called 'hydroponics'.

Scientists are learning how to 'print' food using 3D printers! It is called 3D-printed food. They want to create food that is fresh, natural, delicious, good for the environment and exciting. In the future, they hope to use this technology to help feed many hungry people in the world.

How can you waste less food?

Did you know that a lot of food is thrown away every year? Most of it is still fine to eat. Farmers and supermarkets often throw away fruit and vegetables because they do not look perfect. That food ends up in landfill sites and never gets eaten. At the same time, one in seven people around the world is hungry.

Reduce, Reuse, Recycle

Read this information to learn more about how to be a Green Kid.

Reduce:
Use less of something and do not waste it.

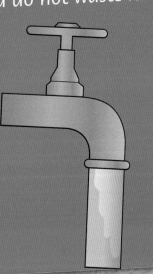

Reuse:
Use things over and over and over again.

Recycle:
Use materials from old things, to make new things.

Being green means ...

- being aware of how everything you do affects our environment
- learning more about how to save our precious resources
- doing your best to protect our Earth.

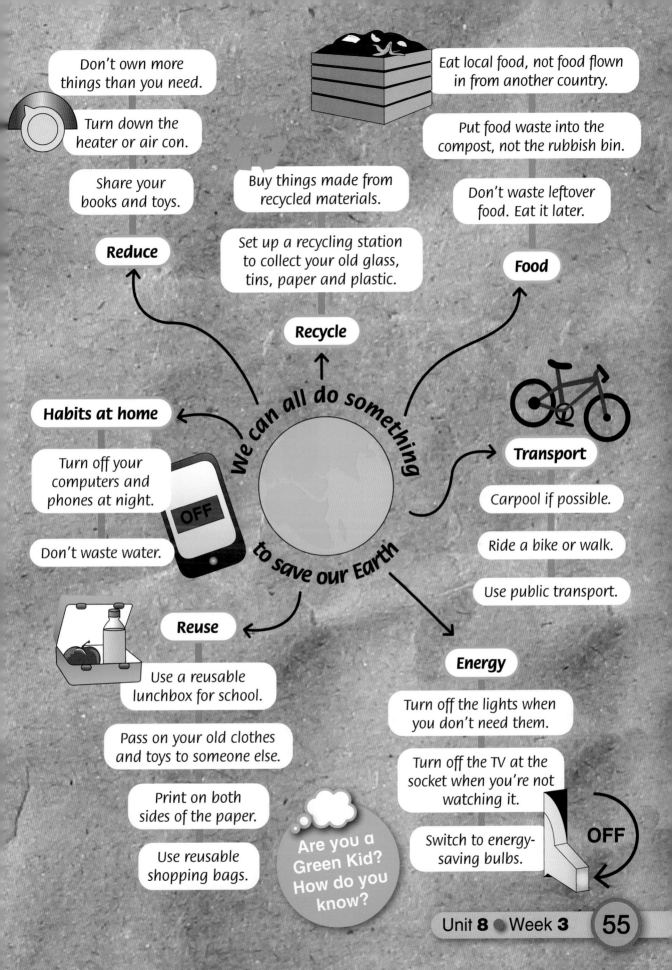

Don't own more things than you need.

Turn down the heater or air con.

Share your books and toys.

Eat local food, not food flown in from another country.

Put food waste into the compost, not the rubbish bin.

Buy things made from recycled materials.

Don't waste leftover food. Eat it later.

Reduce

Set up a recycling station to collect your old glass, tins, paper and plastic.

Food

Recycle

Habits at home

We can all do something

to save our Earth

Transport

Turn off your computers and phones at night.

OFF

Carpool if possible.

Ride a bike or walk.

Don't waste water.

Use public transport.

Reuse

Use a reusable lunchbox for school.

Energy

Pass on your old clothes and toys to someone else.

Turn off the lights when you don't need them.

Print on both sides of the paper.

Turn off the TV at the socket when you're not watching it.

Are you a Green Kid? How do you know?

Switch to energy-saving bulbs.

OFF

Use reusable shopping bags.

Pick a style

Do you dream of being a fashionista … the stylish envy of your peers? This season it's time to reinvent your wardrobe! Read about these different styles. Choose a style. Make a list of what you already have. Make a list of what you still need – then let's go shopping!

Tropical

Summer is on its way and you want to celebrate the sunshine by wearing clothes as bright, colourful, fun and energetic as you are feeling.

What you need: flip flops or sandals; a colourful, summery dress; board shorts or short denim shorts; a loose-fitting shirt; bright jewellery, a large summer hat and a floral scarf to keep the sun off your shoulders; a bright beach bag and large sunglasses.

Hipster

SKATER

You may or may not be a skateboarder, but you want to be both stylish and really comfortable at the same time.

You want to follow the latest fashion trends, but still be unique … outside the cultural norm.

What you need: a stylish hat; large glasses; a checked shirt; skinny jeans; a scarf; sneakers; a knitted cardigan; suspenders (these are called braces in the UK) and a backpack.

What you need: very baggy jeans or loose three-quarter jeans. A loose-fitting T-shirt; a hoodie; cap and skate shoes. Oh yes, and a skateboard, of course.

Which fashion style suits each member in your group? Why?

Funky hair!

Read about Jane. Does she make the right decision?

Jane: Rex, I need your help! Please would you style my hair in a new and funky way, for the school end-of-year party on Saturday?

Rex: Are you sure, Jane? What will your parents say? You ought to ask them first.

Jane: Perhaps you're right … they might not like it. But I want to look more exciting, and this could be a fun surprise for them!

Rex: That's true! We could look at some celebrity magazines to get some ideas.

Jane: Good idea. Which famous actor or singer should I copy!

Rex: Look at this photo… you could have French plaits and look like Amanda Seyfried.

Jane: No, I don't think so. I don't think that style would suit me!

Rex: Well, what about dreadlocks? You could look like Jaden Smith!

Jane: Jaden looks incredible, but I'm not sure that's me!

Rex: All the best people have a fringe now. Look at this photo of Tyra Banks, the supermodel. You could look like her!

Jane: I could never look like her.

Rex: Well, you could have it short. Look at this picture. You would look like the actress Anne Hathaway if you had it short!

Jane: Would I? I'm not sure I would ever look like her … and if you cut it short, it will take a long time to grow again!

Rex: OK, well, you could try ponytails, perhaps? Look at these pictures of actresses Lilly Singh and Lee Yubi. You could copy their style.

Jane: Hmmm. I'm not sure, Rex. Perhaps I shouldn't try to copy a celebrity. Maybe I should create my own style and express myself in my own way. I think I want to look unique and different.

Rex: Yes, you're right. OK, well, what do you want me to do to your hair then?!

Jane: Nothing. I have a great idea. I could wear a wig for the party! Shall I try on one those wigs over there?

Rex: Good idea! How about this one? It's perfect!

Jane: It's brilliant! If I wear this wig, you needn't cut my hair at all!

Do you feel under pressure to look like other people?

How do you express yourself through your personal style?

How to start a fashion blog

So, you want to start your own fashion blog? We have good news for you ... becoming a fashion blogger is simple, easy and cheap. Follow our step-by-step guide and you'll soon be blogging with the best!

fashionblog/howto.com

Step 1: Do your research
Spend some time looking at other fashion blogs. What do you like? What don't you like?

Step 2: Choose a domain
If you want to use your blog to earn money, do not use a free blog-hosting domain. Find a domain that allows you to be the owner of everything you post online. Then choose a great blog name that people can remember.

Step 3: Pick a theme
What will you post on your blog? New fashion? Old fashion? Unusual fashion? Decide what you will do to be unique and to stand out. How will you present your words and pictures to your readers?

Step 4: Get started
Start posting quickly and often. Keep your readers entertained with up-to-date information, pictures and advice.

Step 5: Keep in touch
Your readers will want to know that they are important to you. Ask them questions. Reply to their comments. Start online conversations. Build a fan club of people who enjoy your fashion blog as much as you do.

Marli Starling
@marlistar

I adore your blog! Thanks for your great advice. I'm wearing the clothes you recommended right now and everyone keeps telling me how great I look!

Nikhil Rauli
@nikkirocco

I absolutely love the colours and layout of your blog. Keep up the great work!

Focus on famous people

Read about these people who are famous for different reasons.

J.K. Rowling

This is Joanna Rowling (b. 1965). She is a **famous writer**. She is the author of the popular Harry Potter series. She has sold more than 500 million copies of her books in more than 80 different languages. Some of her books have also been made into movies.

Pablo Picasso

This is Pablo Picasso (1881–1973). He was a **famous artist**. He was a painter, sculptor, poet, playwright and many other things. He painted hundreds of paintings, including *Three Musicians* and *The Weeping Woman*.

Nelson Mandela

This is Nelson Mandela (1918–2013). He was a **famous peacemaker**. He saw that his people were not free to live as they pleased because of their skin colour. He decided to fight for all people to be equal. He became the first black president of South Africa and helped all people to live together peacefully.

Beyoncé Knowles

This is Beyoncé Knowles (b. 1981). She is a **famous musician**. She is a singer, songwriter and actress. She used to sing with the group Destiny's Child, but now she sings solo as Beyoncé. She has sold more than 100 million albums and won more than 15 Grammy Awards.

David Attenborough

This is David Attenborough (b. 1926). He is a famous documentary film maker and naturalist. Three of his most famous documentaries are *The Blue Planet*, *Planet Earth* and *Our Planet*. He shows how amazing nature is and some of the negative effects humans are having on our planet.

Which famous people have you heard of? How do you know about them?

Cristiano Ronaldo

This is Cristiano Ronaldo (b. 1985). He is a **famous sportsman**. He is one of the best professional football players in the world. He has won many awards and has scored many goals for his team.

What does success mean to you?

Read what these teenagers say about success.

I think success means being happy … liking yourself and liking the work you do every day.

If you're famous, you're a success!

For me, success means getting married and having a happy family.

In my opinion, I will feel successful when I own a big house and a nice car.

Success means becoming the boss of my own business.

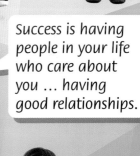

Success is having people in your life who care about you … having good relationships.

I think success is having lots of friends and lots of free time to enjoy life.

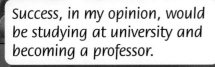

What do you think success is?

Success, I think, is having a great job in a big company and earning lots of money.

Success, in my opinion, would be studying at university and becoming a professor.

For me, if I am healthy, that's success.

William Collins' dream of knowledge for all began with the publication of his first book in 1819. A self-educated mill worker, he not only enriched millions of lives, but also founded a flourishing publishing house. Today, staying true to this spirit, Collins books are packed with inspiration, innovation and practical expertise. They place you at the centre of a world of possibility and give you exactly what you need to explore it.

Collins. Freedom to teach.

An imprint of HarperCollins*Publishers*
The News Building
1 London Bridge Street
London SE1 9GF

HarperCollins*Publishers*
Macken House, 39/40
Mayor Street Upper,
Dublin1, D01 C9W8
Ireland

Browse the complete Collins catalogue at
www.collins.co.uk

ISBN 978-0-00-836915-6

British Library Cataloguing in Publication Data
A catalogue record for this publication is available from the British Library.

Authors: Kathryn Gibbs, Sandy Gibbs, Robert Kellas
Series editor: Daphne Paizee
Publisher: Elaine Higgleton
Product manager: Lucy Cooper
Project manager: Lucy Hobbs
Development editor: Jo Kemp
Proofreader: Sonya Newland
Cover design: Gordon MacGilp
Cover artwork by: DiamondDallas
Internal design by: QBS Learning (SRB and SCB) Hugh Hillyard-Parker and QBS Learning (TG)
Typesetting by: QBS Learning
Illustrations by: QBS Learning
Production controller: Lyndsey Rogers

Printed and bound in India by Replika Press Pvt. Ltd.

MIX
Paper | Supporting
responsible forestry
FSC™ C007454
www.fsc.org

This book is produced from independently certified FSC paper to ensure responsible forest management.

For more information visit: **www.harpercollins.co.uk/green**

With thanks to the following teachers and schools for reviewing materials in development:
Hawar International School; Melissa Brobst, International School of Budapest; Niki Tzorzis, Pascal Primary School Lemessos.

Acknowledgements

The publishers gratefully acknowledge the permissions granted to reproduce copyright material in the book. Every effort has been made to contact the holders of copyright material, but if any have been inadvertently overlooked, the Publisher will be pleased to make the necessary arrangements at the first opportunity.

Extracts on pp.38-39 adapted from 'Every Day is Earth Day on the International Space Station,' 'A Day in the Life Aboard the International Space Station,' 'Christina Koch' and 'Morning Routine in Space'; and the images: The six-member Expedition 61 crew is gathered for a meal, December 31, 2019, https://www.nasa.gov/image-feature/the-six-member-expedition-61-crew-is-gathered-for-a-meal; Christina Koch, December 3, 2018, https://www.nasa.gov/astronauts/biographies/christina-hammock-koch/biography; Spacestation, https://www.nasa.gov/sites/default/files/thumbnails/image/iss056e201248.jpg; Christina Koch and Andrew Morgan, July 23, 2019, https://www.nasa.gov/image-feature/nasa-astronauts-christina-koch-and-andrew-morgan; https://www.nasa.gov/sites/default/files/thumbnails/image/iss060e021613.jpg; and Nap Time on ISS, February 25, 2015, https://www.nasa.gov/image-feature/nap-time-on-iss – source: https://www.nasa.gov/; Image still on p.41 from the video "Refugee Kids: One Small School Takes On The World", http://refugeekidsfilm.com/, copyright © Other Islands Films Inc. Reproduced with permission; Image still on p.41 from the video "Running (Refugee Song)" https://www.youtube.com/watch?v=Rhfo3oBYDPA. This song was released by songwriters and Compositions for a Cause founders Keyon Harrold and Andrea Pizziconi on World Refugee Day. It features Grammy Award-winning singer Gregory Porter, Grammy and Academy Award-winning rapper and actor Common, and Grammy Award-winning trumpeter Keyon Harrold. Reproduced with permission, www.compositionsforacause.com; Book cover image on p.41 from *Four Feet, Two Sandals* by Karen Lynn Williams, copyright © 2007. Reproduced with permission of WM. B. Eerdmans Publishing Co.; SafeWander for 2 photographs on p.47, copyright © SafeWander, www.safewander.com. Reproduced with permission of SensaRx, LLC.; and 'Windmill' figure on p.51, copyright © Tom Reilly, adapted from http://www.solaripedia.com/13/298/3353/william_kamkwamba_windmill_exploded_diagram.html. Used with permission of Moving Windmills Project, Inc.

HarperCollins*Publishers* Limited for extracts and image stills or artwork from:

Elephant's Ears by Grace Webster, illustrated by Emily Golden, text © 2014 Grace Webster. *Harry the Clever Spider on Holiday* by Julia Jarman, illustrated by Charlie Fowkes, text © 2012 Julia Jarman. *The Monster of Pit Street* by Simon Cheshire, illustrated by Keino, text © 2013 Simon Cheshire. *The Hare and the Tortoise* by Melanie Williamson, illustrated by Melanie Williamson, text and artwork © 2013 Melanie Williamson. *Jack and the Beanstalk* by Caryl Hart, illustrated by Nicola L. Robinson, text © 2013 Caryl Hart. *Fishy Friend* by Kipp Whysall, illustrated by Anni Axworthy, text © 2013 Kipp Whysall. *How to Make Storybooks* by Ros Asquith, illustrated by Ros Asquith, text and artwork © 2005 Ros Asquith. *Buried Treasure* by Juliet Kerrigan, illustrated by Fred Blunt, text © 2010 Juliet Kerrigan. *A Day in India* by Jonathan and Angela Scott, text and photography © 2010 Jonathan and Angela Scott. 'I don't know what to do today' from I'm *Growing a Truck in the Garden* by Kenn Nesbitt, text © 2012 Kenn Nesbitt.

Photo acknowledgements

The publishers wish to thank the following for permission to reproduce photographs. Every effort has been made to trace copyright holders and to obtain their permission for the use of copyright materials. The publishers will gladly receive any information enabling them to rectify any error or omission at the first opportunity.

(t = top, c = centre, b = bottom, r = right, l = left)

p4 Monkey Business Images/Shutterstock, p4, 10, 27 (background) 31moonlight31 / Shutterstock, p6, 19-21 (background) SSDDavid /Shutterstock, p7 Monkey Business Images/Shutterstock, p10b wavebreakmedia/Shutterstock, p11 (background) Leona Kali/Shutterstock, p13 (background) Chinch/Shutterstock, p18 (background) Kir_Prime/Shutterstock, p24tl Spreadthesign/Shutterstock, p24r Ilya Bolotov/Shutterstock, p24bl, 24br Rvector/Shutterstock, p25tr Chronicle/Mary Evans/Alamy, p25c KGPA Ltd/Alamy, p25br Bettmann/Getty, p25 (background) Peter Cripps/Shutterstock, p26 tr andrey_l/Shutterstock, p26brPavel Tvrdy/Shutterstock, p27t martinho Smart/Shutterstock, p27c Tereza Kotkova, p27b Kernel Nguyen, p28 (background) Ekaphon maneechot/Shutterstock, p30 (background) Alleksander/Shutterstock, p30t DiamondDallas/Shutterstock, p30c weerasak saeku/Shutterstock, p30b SNEHIT/Shutterstock, p31t HelloRF Zcool/Shutterstock, p32tl Palladin/Shutterstock, p32tr tsuneomp/Shutterstock, p32bl kamomeen/Shutterstock, p32bc Lijphoto/Shutterstock, p32br Concept Photo/Shutterstock, p33tl Guzsudio/Shutterstock, p33tr BonnieBC/Shutterstock, p33cr Andrei Medvedev/Shutterstock, p33bl Stuart Monk/Shutterstock, p33br Susan Law Cain/Shutterstock, p34 (background) Tupungato/Shutterstock, p35tr Andaman/Shutterstock, p35l Andrew V Marcus/Shutterstock, p35b AnjelikaGr/Shutterstock, p35br Genevieve Vallee/Alamy, p36tl ducu59us/Shutterstock, p36c, 36b Matjazz/Shutterstock, p37t gary corbett/Alamy, p37b Randy Duchaine/Alamy, pp38-39 (background) KPP/Shutterstock, p40t Giannis Papanikos/Shutterstock, p40b thomas koch/Shutterstock, p40 (background) Tolga Sezgin/Shutterstock, p41t © Other Islands Films, p41c songwriters and Compositions for a Cause founders Keyon Harrold and Andrea Pizziconi, p41b WM. B. Eerdmans Publishing Co. , p42t Ververidis Vasilis/Shutterstock, p42b Nice_Media/Shutterstock, p42 (background) Procyk Radek/Shutterstock, p43 (background) Africa Studio/Shutterstock, p44t Istry Istry/Shutterstock, p44l wavebreakmedia/Shutterstock, p44r wavebreakmedia/Shutterstock, p44 (background) RomanR/Shutterstock, p45t Photographee.eu/Shutterstock, p45c Prometheus72/Shutterstock, p45b Sergey Nivens/Shutterstock, p46t photonic 7/Alamy, p46b © ManCans, p47t Mike Pont/Getty, p47c © SafeWander, p47b © SafeWander, p47 (background) RedlineVector/Shutterstock, p48 (background) Rawpixel.com/Shutterstock, p49l StockLite /Shutterstock, p49c Artem Shadrin/Shutterstock, p49r Monkey Business Images/Shutterstock, p50 (background) XXLPhoto/Shutterstock, p51 Lucas Oleniuk/Getty, p52t Nopparat Nakhamhom/Shutterstock, p52b bunyarit/Shutterstock, p52 (background) Vlad Teodor/Shutterstock, p53t Alex_Traksel/Shutterstock, p53c Heike Rau/Shutterstock, p53b Michele Paccione/Shutterstock, p54 (background) autsawin uttisin/Shutterstock, p56 (men's outfit) nataliakul/Shutterstock, p56 (sandals) Harry Cabance/Shutterstock, p56 (scarf) Andrienko Anastasiya/Shutterstock, p56 (flip flops) Serhii Tsyhanok/Shutterstock, p56 (bag) atyana Vyc/Shutterstock, p56 (bangles) Michael Kraus/Shutterstock, p56 (dress) Tarzhanova/Shutterstock, p56 (sunglasses) Dima Moroz/Shutterstock, p56 (hat) Bunwit Unseree/Shutterstock, p56 (background) Bohbeh/Shutterstock, p57 (hipster top) Evgeniya Porechenskaya/Shutterstock, p57 (red backpack) mihgli/Shutterstock, p57 (red braces) Vitalii Gorbatiuk/Shutterstock, p57 (hipster bottom) Floral Deco/Shutterstock, p57 (black hat) Mega Pixel/Shutterstock, p57 (black bag) sasha_nkpl/Shutterstock, p57 (female shoes) nikki / Shutterstock.com/Shutterstock, p57 (female jeans) elenovsky/Shutterstock, p57 (cardigan) siSSen/Shutterstock, p57 (skater top) ONNINSTUDIO/Shutterstock, p57 (skater bottom) Who is Danny/Shutterstock, p58 (background) Champ008/Shutterstock, p58tl Dimitrios Kambouris/Getty, p58t Jim Spellman/Getty, p58tr Randy Brooke/Getty, p58bl Kevin Winter /Getty, p58b Han Myung-Gu/Getty, p58br Noam Galai /Getty, p60t goodluz/Shutterstock, p60b Rawpixel.com/Shutterstock, p60 (background0 Africa Studio/Shutterstock, p61tl Everett Collection/Shutterstock, p61tr Mashka/Shutterstock, p61cl Keystone Pictures USA/Alamy, p61cr Mira/Alamy, p61b Alessia Pierdomenico/Shutterstock, p62tr Tonya Wise/Shutterstock, p62ct Jason Batterham/Alamy, p62cb Digital Images Studio, p62b Marcos Mesa Sam Wordley/Shutterstock, p63a mimagephotography/Shutterstock, p63b Creativa Images/Shutterstock, p63c Hugo Felix/Shutterstock, p63d Darrin Henry/Shutterstock, p63e kurhan NONWARIT/Shutterstock, p63f kurhan/Shutterstock, p63g luckyraccoon/Shutterstock, p63h Monsterstock/Shutterstock, p63i Hogan Imaging/Shutterstock, p63j PORTRAIT IMAGES ASIA BY NONWARIT/Shutterstock, p63 (background) Leona Kali/Shutterstock